Lerner SPORTS

SPORTS ALL-STARS

PAUL GEORGE

Jon M. Fishman

Lerner Publications ◆ Minneapolis

Lerner Publications Company
An imprint of Lerner Publishing Group, Inc.
241 First Avenue North
Minneapolis, MN 55401 USA

For reading levels and more information, look up this title at www.lernerbooks.com.

Main body text set in Albany Std 22. Typeface provided by Agfa.

Editor: Rebecca Higgins **Designer:** Viet Chu **Photo Editor:** Brianna Kaiser

Library of Congress Cataloging-in-Publication Data

Names: Fishman, Jon M., author.
Title: Paul George / Jon M. Fishman.
Description: Minneapolis : Lerner Publications, 2021. | Series: Sports all-stars | Includes bibliographical references and index. | Audience: Ages 7–11 | Audience: Grades 2–3 | Summary: "Los Angeles Clippers shooting guard and small forward Paul George dominated six All-Star Games. He was selected for five All-NBA Teams and four NBA All-Defensive Teams. Get to know this basketball star!"— Provided by publisher.
Identifiers: LCCN 2019052420 (print) | LCCN 2019052421 (ebook) | ISBN 9781541597532 (library binding) | ISBN 9781728414065 (paperback) | ISBN 9781728401027 (ebook)
Subjects: LCSH: George, Paul, 1990—Juvenile literature. | Basketball players—United States—Biography—Juvenile literature.
Classification: LCC GV884.G46 F57 2021 (print) | LCC GV884.G46 (ebook) | DDC 796.323092 [B]—dc23

LC record available at https://lccn.loc.gov/2019052420
LC ebook record available at https://lccn.loc.gov/2019052421

Manufactured in the United States of America
1-47857-48297-9/28/2020

CONTENTS

PLAYOFF P

Paul George lines up a shot in 2019.

The season was on the line for Paul George and the Oklahoma City Thunder. In the first round of the 2019 National Basketball Association (NBA) playoffs, George and

FACTS AT A GLANCE

- **Date of birth:** May 2, 1990
- **Position:** **forward**, shooting guard
- **League:** NBA
- **Professional highlights:** chosen 10th overall by the Indiana Pacers in the 2010 NBA Draft; overcame a serious leg injury in 2014; led the 2016 NBA All-Star Game with 41 points
- **Personal highlights:** learned to play basketball at parks and at home with his sisters; loves fishing; has two dogs, King and Kobe

George hustles after a loose ball.

his teammates trailed Portland three games to one. One more loss would end Oklahoma City's season. But the Thunder had Playoff P.

Playoff P is a nickname George gave himself. During the regular season, he's one of the NBA's best players. During the playoffs as Playoff P, he dominates the court.

George wasted no time becoming his **persona**, Playoff P. In the opening seconds of the game, he dribbled the ball down the court. Suddenly, he stopped and took a long three-point shot. *Swish!* The score gave the Thunder a 3–0 lead.

At the other end of the court, the Trail Blazers missed a three-pointer. George reached and grabbed the **rebound**. It was just the beginning of a huge night for the Oklahoma City forward.

George led the Thunder to a 37–29 lead by the end of

the first quarter. But the cheering Portland fans inspired the Trail Blazers. They surged from behind to win the game, 118–115. Oklahoma City's season was finished.

Despite losing in the playoffs, George ended the game with 36 points, nine rebounds, and three **assists**. George is one of the league's best scorers and defenders, but he wants more than personal success. His goal is to win the top NBA title. "The most important thing is winning a championship," he said.

George plays tough defense against Portland's Damian Lillard.

AT HOME ON THE COURT

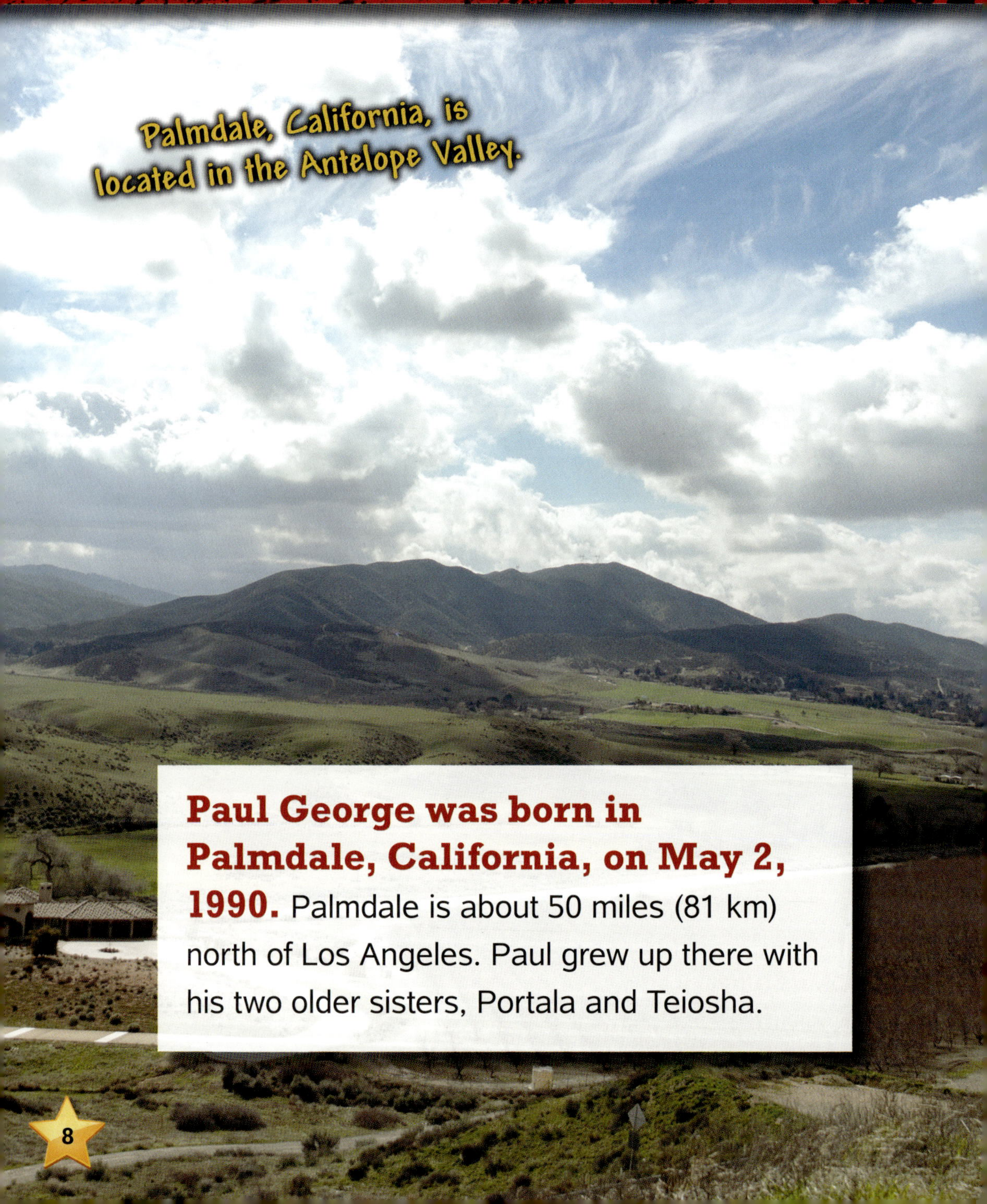

Palmdale, California, is located in the Antelope Valley.

Paul George was born in Palmdale, California, on May 2, 1990. Palmdale is about 50 miles (81 km) north of Los Angeles. Paul grew up there with his two older sisters, Portala and Teiosha.

Paul grew up with a love of basketball.

Palmdale didn't offer many ways to entertain kids. Sometimes Paul went bowling or saw a movie with his family. But most of the time, he played basketball.

At home, Paul played with a **portable** basketball hoop. He and his sisters would drag it into the street to play. When he wasn't at home, he shot baskets with his friends at Domenic Massari Park. The park had a gray-and-white court with metal **backboards**.

Later, Paul played at Palmdale's Knight High School. He loved basketball so much that he wanted to play all

George pushes past a defender in 2010.

the time. Knight's basketball coach, Tom Hegre, often left the gym open after school for Paul and his friends. They played for hours, running up and down the court. "It became like their home away from home," Hegre said. When it got too late, the coach would kick the kids out and close the gym.

The practice paid off. Paul's points, assists, and rebounds per game rose each year at Knight. As a senior, he averaged more than 23 points and 11 rebounds per game. He won the 2008 Golden League Most Valuable Player award.

After high school, George attended California State University, Fresno, in central California. He made a big impact as a college freshman with more than 14 points and six rebounds per game. But the team had a losing record

Paul was the best player in his league in the 2007–2008 season. But California is a huge state with many great players. When Paul graduated from Knight in 2008, he was the 20th-ranked high school player in the state.

George reaches for a dunk against the Chicago Bulls.

and finished ninth in their **conference**. Almost all of George's stats improved in his second season. But the team didn't do much better. George was ready to move on.

NBA **scouts** loved George's size. He stood 6 feet 9 inches (2 m) tall and weighed almost 215 pounds (98 kg). They were less sure about his basketball history. How good could he be after playing on a losing team?

The Indiana Pacers believed in George. They chose him with the 10th overall pick in the 2010 NBA Draft. He set out to prove that the nine teams that didn't pick him had made a mistake.

BACK FROM A BREAK

George scored 1,737 points in the 2013–2014 season.

George's scoring ability and tough defense made him one of the league's most valuable players. In 2013–2014, he played in his second All-Star Game and led the

George drives past James Harden during a 2014 practice game with the US national team.

Pacers to the Eastern Conference Finals. Fans couldn't wait to see how far the team could go next season.

On August 1, 2014, in Las Vegas, Nevada, everything changed. While playing in a practice game for the United States national team, George soared to block a shot. When he landed, he fell to the court in pain. He left the arena in an ambulance with a leg injury.

Both of the bones in George's lower right leg were broken. The injury was severe. Doctors knew his bones would recover but were worried about his muscles. On August 2, he had surgery to repair the bones.

Fans, coaches, and players wished George a fast recovery on social media. "Thanks everybody for the love and support," he posted on Twitter. "I'll be OK and [I'll] be back better than ever!!!"

About two months after his surgery, George was back on his feet. Doctors told him he could begin to work out. But it would be a long time before his leg would be strong

George worked hard to recover from his injury.

George eats nuts as a snack before dinner.

enough to play in the NBA. Many people expected him to miss the entire 2014–2015 season.

Five days a week, George worked to return to the Pacers. He started by lifting weights with his upper body. He shot baskets wearing a special **walking boot** to protect his lower leg.

To fuel his recovery, George began eating more healthful foods. “Once I changed my diet I noticed I had a ton of energy—I was more lively and ready for the workouts, my body was better,” he said. He eats healthful foods such as eggs, green beans, nuts, and chicken.

As his bones healed, George began to practice with his teammates again. He played in six games for the Pacers at the end of the 2014–2015 season. He averaged just 8.8 points. But in 2015–2016, he proved he was still a fierce competitor. In February, George played in his third All-Star Game. He led all players in the game with 41 points.

George dribbles down the court in the 2016 All-Star Game.

FISHING AND FRIENDS

George casts out his line at the Paul George Celebrity Fishing Tournament.

George stayed active after his surgery by playing golf.

George's broken leg kept him off the court for almost a full season. He had a lot of other interests to focus on as he healed. Wearing a walking boot, George went golfing just weeks after surgery. He also took part in one of his favorite activities: fishing.

As a kid, George learned to fish from his dad. They

George reels in a catch during his fishing tournament.

bonded over the activity. George loves the peace and quiet of being on a boat and casting out his line. After his surgery, fishing helped him stay busy until he could play basketball again.

Every summer, George hosts the Paul George Celebrity Fishing Tournament. Teammates, friends, and celebrities hit the lake to see who can reel in the biggest catch. The tournament raises money for athletic equipment in Palmdale and other good causes. George also hopes the event creates new fishing fans.

he did was play basketball with his dog. George's daughter, Olivia, also loves King. "It's pretty awesome to see her bond with a dog," he said.

In 2016, George welcomed a new dog to the family. He named the new addition Kobe, after NBA legend Kobe Bryant. Olivia and Kobe bonded right away.

George and Kobe Bryant smile after competing against each other in 2015. George named one of his dogs after the basketball legend.

George presents a check to Palmdale's Department of Recreation and Culture.

In 2018, George gave $25,000 to Palmdale to upgrade city parks. The improvement projects might include Domenic Massari Park, where George played as a kid. He also gave money to Knight High School for their gym. Among the improvements are brand-new glass backboards, just like they use in the NBA.

George's NBA earnings allow him to give back to his community. Through the 2019–2020 season, he has earned about $145 million playing basketball. He also makes money **endorsing** products from companies such as Nike and Gatorade. In 2019, *Forbes* magazine said George was the 33rd highest-paid athlete in the world.

George speaks at a Nike press conference.

HOME AGAIN

George looks for an open teammate in 2017.

George was set to become a free agent after the 2017–2018 season. That meant he would be able to join any NBA team. He liked playing in Indiana. But he missed Southern California.

George guards Victor Oladipo of the Indiana Pacers.

If George left for a new team after the season, the Pacers would be left with nothing in return for their star player. Instead, they traded him to Oklahoma City in June 2017.

The Thunder had a winning record in 2017–2018. But in June 2018, George again expressed his wish to play in the Los Angeles area. “Everyone in the league would say that they would love to go back home and play for their city,” George said. “It’s just something about representing home.”

Going for Gold

After healing from his broken leg, George rejoined the US national team. In 2016, George and the United States won the gold medal in men's basketball at the Olympic Games in Rio de Janeiro, Brazil.

George (*top right*) celebrates a gold medal win with the 2016 US national team.

In July 2019, the Thunder made his wish come true by trading him to the Los Angeles Clippers. He joined fellow superstar Kawhi Leonard to form one of the NBA's most fearsome teams. It's only a matter of time before George wins a championship for his hometown fans.

George is determined to win with his home team.

Glossary

assists: passes that lead to scores

backboards: rounded or rectangular boards behind the baskets on basketball courts

conference: a group of teams that play against one another

endorsing: recommending a product or service, usually in exchange for money

forward: a player who usually plays at the front of a team's formation near the opponent's basket

persona: a personality that a person uses in public

portable: capable of being carried or moved about

rebound: an instance of grabbing and controlling the ball after a missed shot

scouts: people who judge the skills of athletes

walking boot: a stiff plastic boot used to protect an injured foot or lower leg

Source Notes

7 "Paul George: Winning a Title 'Most Important Thing' in Free Agency Decision," NBA, June 29, 2018, https://www.nba.com/article/2018/06/29/paul-george-championship-focus-driving-decision-free-agency-2018.

10 Tania Ganguli, "For Paul George, L.A. Homecoming Transcends the Business of Basketball," *Los Angeles Times*, February 16, 2018, https://www.latimes.com/sports/nba/la-sp-paul-george-profile-20170216-story.html.

15 Ben Golliver, "Pacers' Paul George Suffers Severe Leg Fracture at USA Basketball Showcase," *Sports Illustrated*, August 2, 2014, https://www.si.com/nba/2014/08/02/paul-george-leg-surgery-indiana-pacers.

16 Luke Darby, "The Real-Life Diet of Paul George, Who Made the Comeback of the Year," *Gentlemen's Quarterly*, April 12, 2016, https://www.gq.com/story/paul-george-real-life-diet.

21 Peter Walsh, "This Is for My Dogs," *Slam*, March 6, 2017, https://www.slamonline.com/nba/this-is-for-my-dogs/.

25 "Paul George: Winning a Title."

Further Information

Fishman, Jon M. *Kawhi Leonard.* Minneapolis: Lerner Publications, 2018.

Flynn, Brendan. *Los Angeles Clippers All-Time Greats.* Mankato, MN: Press Box Books, 2020.

Jr. NBA
https://jr.nba.com/

Levit, Joe. *Basketball's G.O.A.T.: Michael Jordan, LeBron James, and More.* Minneapolis: Lerner Publications, 2020.

Los Angeles Clippers
https://www.nba.com/clippers/

Paul George
https://www.nba.com/players/paul/george/202331

Index

Photo Acknowledgments

Image credits: Steve Dykes/Getty Images, pp. 4, 6, 7; Dylan Gemora/Shutterstock, p. 8; RyanJLane/Getty Images, p. 9; Eric Paul Zamora/Fresno Bee/Tribune News Service/Getty Images, p. 10; Chris Sweda/Chicago Tribune/Tribune News Service/Getty Images, p. 12; Andy Lyons/Getty Images, pp. 13, 15, 25; Ethan Miller/Getty Images, p. 14; Eugenia Lucasenco/Shutterstock.com, p. 16; Elsa/Getty Images, p. 17; Cassy Athena/Getty Images, pp. 18, 20, 22; Dan Thornberg/Shutterstock.com, p. 19; Kevork Djansezian/Getty Images, p. 21; Mark Fredesjed R. Cristino/Pacific Press/LightRocket/Getty Images, p. 23; Sean Gardner/Getty Images, p. 24; Mark Ralston/AFP/Getty Images, p. 26; John McCoy/Getty Images, p. 27.

Cover: Andy Lyons/Getty Images.